Inspiring
Women
Every Day

GW00854116

Plus … Special Article, Ministry Report and CWR Events Page

MIX
Paper from
responsible sources
FSC® C015900

DEBBIE LAYCOCK

Debbie Laycock (nee Forster, married to Joe in 2007) graduated from Cambridge in Classics and then worked for two years with an evangelistic youth project in inner-city London. She later trained in theology, church leadership and church planting with Ichthus Christian Fellowship where she has worked ever since. Today she serves on the central Ministry and Management Team of Ichthus, and also manages the Ichthus Training Programmes. She teaches New Testament Greek, some theology and holds a certificate in Ancient Near Eastern Languages, majoring on Biblical Hebrew. She is also proud to be a trustee of Know Your Bible.

REBECCA LOWE

Rebecca Lowe, 38, is a writer, speaker and media consultant, based in Swansea, south Wales. She graduated from Oxford with a degree in Theology, then worked as a journalist, becoming freelance following the birth of her daughter, Stephanie. She has written for a wide range of religious and secular organisations, including editing newsletters for Care for the Family. Married to Rob, she also acts as a volunteer media officer for the Christian relief and development agency, Tearfund.

Copyright © CWR 2012. Published by CWR, Waverley Abbey House, Waverley Lane, Farnham, Surrey GU9 8EP, UK. Tel: 01252 784700 Email: mail@cwr.org.uk Registered Charity No. 294387. Registered Limited Company No. 1990308.

Front cover image: getty/Eric Audras. Concept development, editing, design and production by CWR. Printed in England by Linney Print. All rights reserved. No part of this publication may be reproduced, stored in a retrieval system, or transmitted, in any form or by any means, electronic, mechanical, photocopying, recording or otherwise, without the prior permission in writing of CWR.

Unless otherwise indicated, all Scripture references are from the Holy Bible: New International Version (NIV), copyright © 1979, 1984, 2011 by Biblica (formerly International Bible Society). Used by permission of Hodder & Stoughton Publishers, an Hachette UK company. All rights reserved.

Any other Bible versions used:

HCSB: Holman Christian Standard Bible®, Copyright © 1999, 2000, 2002, 2003 by Holman Bible Publishers. Used by permission. Holman Christian Standard Bible®, Homan CSB®, and HCSB® are federally registered trademarks of Holman Bible Publishers.

NASB: New American Standard Bible. Scripture taken from the NEW AMERICAN STANDARD BIBLE®, Copyright © 1960, 1962, 1963, 1968, 1971, 1972, 1973, 1975, 1977, 1995 by the Lockman Foundation. Used by permission.

WEEKEND

Jonah and Nahum

For reflection: Jonah 4:1–2; Nahum 1:3
'The LORD is slow to anger …' (Nahum 1:3; Jonah 4:2)

'A rose by any other name would smell as sweet', wrote Shakespeare. True, but if we called it a stink-blossom, we might question the name's appropriateness!

Jonah and Nahum were the two prophets to Nineveh recorded in the Bible. Jonah prophesied the city's destruction in the eighth century BC but, because the people repented, God relented. Around 150 years later, Nahum also prophesied Nineveh's destruction, only this time it was shortly fulfilled; in 612 BC the city fell.

'Jonah' means 'dove', the symbol of peace after judgment; 'Nahum' means 'comfort'. God chose prophets with awkwardly inappropriate names for the messages He wanted them to deliver! Jonah heralded the *beginning* of a judgment that never took place; Nahum detailed God's *anger* towards Nineveh. 'Jonah' and 'Nahum' remind us to look to Jesus for a full understanding of God's Old Testament judgment. Jesus was the One on whom the Spirit's *dove* rested; the One who *comforted* the mourners; the One who took mankind's wickedness and God's judgment to the cross and made an end of it there so we could know His peace and mercy eternally.

Optional further reading
Numbers 14:17–18; Genesis 6:1–9,17; 1 Peter 3:18–22; John 1:29–34; Matthew 5:4

No guts, **no glory!**

'But Jonah ran away from the LORD ...' (v.3)

Jonah's is a gutsy story: his lack of guts initially meant fish guts for him later on! Following the Lord requires some courage; we don't always feel we have what it takes. In this passage, the Hebrew translation literally says God was looking for some 'get up and go!' And Jonah did, in the opposite direction! If he hadn't turned around, we'd never have seen the glory of a whole city turning to the Lord. Don't you long to see your hometown respond so wholeheartedly to God?

My father once knew a man who joined an evangelistic team. Every day for a week they entertained people with songs, puppets and testimonies, promoting a gospel event at the weekend. On the last day it was *his* turn to share a testimony. Being terribly shy, it filled him with dread, but he wanted to be obedient. He stumbled and stuttered his way through, brow sweating, knees knocking, nervously wringing his hands behind his back. A lady was standing behind him keeping an eye on her child. She couldn't hear a word of the man's faltering testimony, but she saw his hands wringing, his knees knocking and the sweat pouring. 'If he's willing to put himself through all that, he must believe his message is really important!' she thought. So she went along to the gospel meeting, met Jesus and entrusted her life to Him.

That man heard Jesus' call, gathered some guts and took a step of obedience. The result was a life changed by Jesus. Don't let fear rob you of the glory the Lord wants to display through your life. We only need enough guts to get up and take *a step* in the right direction; then the Lord meets us there and fills our feeble efforts with His glorious accomplishments.

For prayer and reflection

Are you running away from something Jesus is calling you to do? Pray: Lord, fill me with courage to obey You. Use me to bring glory to You where I live. Amen.

Kept **in the dark**

'How can you
sleep? Get up and
call on your god!'
(v.6)

ndian folklore tells a story of six blind men asked
to describe what an elephant is like. One touches
the ear and says 'a fan'; one touches the leg and
says 'a pillar'; one touches the tail and says 'a rope' and
so on. All are right, though none has the whole truth.

A friendly lady at my church outreach said 'Although
I'm a devout Muslim, I'm glad you're telling people
about Jesus. It's good for people to have a moral code
to live by, whichever religion they choose.' I had a
choice: spoil the conversation by contradicting her,
explaining why Jesus is *the* One to follow, or remain
on common ground by simply nodding my agreement.
Before I could respond she had to go; but what would
Jesus have said to her?

And what would Jesus say to my Muslim friend
describing how, even through ceremonial washings, she
could never feel clean before God? Or to the spiritualist,
trying to ease her grief by contacting her dead mother,
and now plagued by bad dreams and hauntings? To the
atheist in despair because he'd no one to forgive his life's
mistakes? Jesus wouldn't leave them bound up in false
beliefs; He came to give life in all its fullness, truth to set
them free and a way to love God and be loved by Him.

Has fear of disturbing the peace led the Church to
quietly slumber, like Jonah in the bottom of the boat,
leaving people to grope for answers in the dark? Have
we accepted the elephant parable, allowing others
to navigate the storms of life calling on gods who can
neither hear nor save? The sailors shook Jonah awake,
firing their questions at him in desperation for their lives
before he spoke up for his God. Let's not keep people in
the dark about Jesus' saving power!

**For prayer and
reflection**

**Lord, show me
something fresh
today about the
uniqueness of
Jesus. Give me
an opportunity
to share it with
someone who
needs to know
Your saving
power. Amen.**

A man **before his time**

Jonah 1:9–10

'... I worship the
LORD, the God of
heaven, who made
the sea and the
dry land.' (v.9)

Humans are insecure creatures. Forgetting we're all made in God's image, we resort to exclusivity, adopting 'us and them' mentalities to control others and boost ourselves.

A Christian friend once told me we couldn't be friends any more because she'd heard that my father, a well-known Bible teacher, held 'heretical' views on hell. 'How could our unity in the faith, our fellowship in the Spirit, possibly depend on what *my dad* might believe?' I thought. We huddle in our theologically distinctive camps, not always out of passion for the truth, but because it gives us a fleshly confidence, sadly not based in Christ.

In Jonah's time, the Israelites believed that God was *their* God and that, as His special possession, He stood up for Israel; their enemies were His. True, only they could fulfil His unique purpose: to bring forth Jesus. But through Jesus, God had an *even more wonderful plan*: to draw people of every tribe, tongue and nation.

The apostle Paul marvelled at this revelation of God's universal love; uncovering the mystery that Jesus died to reconcile Gentiles to God, as well as Jews. He enthuses, '... the Gentiles are fellow heirs, fellow members of the body, fellow partakers of the promise in Christ Jesus' (Eph. 3:6, NASB).

How marvellous that Jonah got hold of God's heart for the world: he knew God had made the whole earth; He knew God wanted to save him *and* the idol-worshipping sailors; he knew God wanted to show mercy even to the wicked people of Nineveh. He gave us a preview of God's heart as we would see it revealed in Jesus. Jonah was a man before his time.

For prayer and reflection

Think of someone you find it hard to imagine belonging to the family of God. Pray that Jesus will wash away wrong judgments and give you His heart of love for them.

Cross purposes

Jonah 1:11–15

'Instead, the men did their best to row back to land. But they could not …' (v.13)

Angela was depressed with a serious gambling addiction; social services threatened to take away her children. I visited her weekly to talk and pray, encouraging her to come to the cross for forgiveness and a new start. She'd say 'Just let me get myself sorted out first. Once I've stopped gambling, paid my debts and set my home in order, *then* I'll come to God.'

Even as Christians, we can try to avoid the cross. The powers of sin and Satan buffet us like stormy seas, driving us further away from God's purposes. Yet, like the sailors, we'd rather find our *own way* back to solid ground. We row as hard as we can, we try to change, to become something God could be pleased with. We close off our hearts from engaging with Jesus in repentance and worship.

There are two ways of understanding the cross: 1. It changed something in God's heart by appeasing His wrath against sinful mankind (propitiation). 2. It changed something in our hearts by cleansing us from sin, removing its stain (expiation). Jonah's story shows us both. Jonah saw himself as an expiatory sacrifice: *his* sin was causing the storm; if he died, the sin would be removed (v.12). The sailors saw him as a propitiatory sacrifice: his death might please God, appeasing His wrath and calming the storm (v.14).

If we want to be rid of our sin and please God, we have to come to the cross, where Christ was made sin for us and where the Father was pleased with His Son's perfect obedience. As Angela discovered, our best efforts will never bring us closer to God. Her life only turned around when she finally surrendered it at the cross.

For prayer and reflection

Lord, thank You for the cross. Show me where I am striving in my own strength and deliver me by Your power, so I can be cleansed and renewed to please You. Amen.

Going **down?**

Jonah 1:16–17

'… and Jonah was in the belly of the fish …' (v.17)

While preaching at another church, the Lord gave me a word of knowledge. It referred to a children's book, a favourite of the person whom the word was for, and described how she'd woken up that morning feeling at rock-bottom and asked herself 'How did I get here?' Afterwards, a lady came to me in tears, saying 'That's me! A year ago I made a decision with my life that I knew was not what God wanted for me. Since then I've been sinking lower and lower. Today I woke up and realised I was depressed; but it was only when you shared that word that I realised *where* it all started to go wrong.'

Jonah's story follows a similar pattern. Did you notice in this chapter how many times he 'goes down'? The Hebrew text shows it best: Jonah ran away *down* to Joppa (v.3); he got *down* into the ship (v.3); he went *down* below deck (v.5); and he lay *down* to sleep (v.5). On top of that, he was thrown down into the sea and swallowed down into a fish's belly. He couldn't have got much lower! Turning away from the Lord started him on a downward spiral. He was so low he even slept through a raging storm. In Romans 1:21, Paul describes a society that had rejected God in terms of its 'futile thinking' and 'darkened hearts'. There are many reasons for depression, but one spiritual factor can be that, like Jonah, we're running away from God.

God's command to Jonah was 'Go' – literally 'arise!' (v.2). We're then told twice that he 'ran away from the LORD' (vv.3,10) and began his descent. To get back on the up again, he'd have to return to the Lord; and, when he did, he found Him gracious, compassionate, slow to anger and abounding in love.

For prayer and reflection

Reflect: Am I in a downward spiral, or are things looking up? Am I where the Lord wants me to be? Is my next step in life taking me nearer to the Lord or further away from Him?

CWR MINISTRY EVENTS

Please pray for the team

Date	Event	Place	Presenter(s)
4 Sep	Insight into Bereavement	Waverley Abbey House	Peter Jackson
6 Sep	Discovering Your Spiritual Gifts	WAH	Andy Peck
8 Sep	Insight into Depression	Pilgrim Hall	Chris Ledger
11 Sep	Discovering More About God's Story	WAH	Philip Greenslade
13 Sep	Reaching Teenagers	WAH	Andy Peck & Martin Saunders
15 Sep	Understanding Yourself, Understanding Others (MBTI® Basic)	WAH	Lynn & Andrew Penson
20 Sep	Bible in a Day	WAH	Andy Peck
26 Sep	Help! I Want to Read the Bible (FREE EVENT)	WAH	Andy Peck & Lynette Brooks
28 Sep	Career Changes and Choices	WAH	Stephen & Rosalyn Derges
28-30 Sep	Women's Weekend: 'In His Presence'	WAH	Lynn Penson & Rosalyn Derges
5-7 Oct	Bible Discovery Weekend: 'David - the Man After God's Own Heart'	WAH	Philip Greenslade
5 Oct	Insight into Depression	WAH	Chris Ledger
6 Oct	Women's Autumn Day: 'Trust in the Lord with All Your Heart'	WAH	Lynn Penson
7 Oct	Prayer Evening	WAH	Canon Andrew White tbc
8 Oct	Developing Pastoral Care (Part 1)	WAH	Andy Peck, Philip Greenslade, Lynn Penson & team
10 Oct	Small Group Leaders' Toolbox	Pilgrim Hall	Andy Peck
14 Oct	Depression and Anxiety - Helping Teenagers with Hidden Problems	WAH	Chris Ledger
17 Oct	Personality and Spirituality	WAH	Lynn & Andrew Penson

Please also pray for students and tutors on our ongoing **BA in Counselling** programme at Waverley and our **Certificate and Diploma of Christian Counselling** and **MA in Integrative Psychotherapy** held at London School of Theology.

For full details phone 01252 784719, international +44 (0)1252 784719
or see the CWR website for further information www.cwr.org.uk

WEEKEND

The sign of Jonah

For reflection: Matthew 16:1–4; Luke 11:28–32; Matthew 12:39–41
'… now one greater than Jonah is here.'
(Matt. 12:41; Luke 11:32)

J onah gets a bad press as a rather grumpy and difficult prophet. Yet he's the only prophet that Jesus explicitly identifies Himself with.

In Matthew 16:4, the *sign* is to point people to repentance and faith. As soon as the Ninevites saw Jonah, spat up on the seashore, oozing with gastric juices and stinking of fish, they hastened to repent, putting their faith in the Lord's mercy. In contrast, Jesus lamented that His generation refused to recognise the sign of His coming and would not repent.

In Luke 11:32, Jonah was a *sign*, but also a *parallel* for Jesus' preaching. When Jonah prophesied, Nineveh listened and responded, but Jesus' contemporaries closed their ears and hardened their hearts to His challenging words. In Matthew 12:40, Jesus points to repentance and faith; Jonah's prophecy *parallels* Jesus' preaching; but he's also a *type*, foreshadowing Jesus' death, burial and resurrection through his experiences in the fish's belly.

Jesus can use even grumpy and difficult people like us to point others to Him: in our lives, our words and *even* our failures and pressures.

Optional further reading
1 Corinthians 1:20–31; 2 Corinthians12:1–10; Hebrews 1:1–4

Low point or **turning point?**

'From inside the fish Jonah prayed to the LORD his God.' (v.1)

A friend once observed that people are characterised by the 'reflex' prayers they most often pray. Les Isaac, founder of Street Pastors, prayed every day 'Lord, make me a righteous man'; today he floods our cities with that righteousness. As soon as he wakes up, my dad prays 'Lord, fill me with Your Spirit'; he's a Spirit-filled man. When I asked myself this question, I decided that I most often prayed 'Lord, help me!' and, although He graciously did as I lurched from one crisis to the next, it left me wondering why my prayer life was so disaster-driven. I resolved to spend more time listening to the Lord for my day rather than waiting until I was in trouble to pray.

Only at his lowest point does Jonah talk to God. Swallowed by a sea-monster, unsurprisingly he's 'in distress' and wonders if he might be dead. From Jonah's perspective things couldn't get any worse; but from God's, *this* was Jonah's salvation. The fish saved him from drowning! Now, Jonah's life could make a U-turn.

In our deepest despair we often go deepest with God; with nowhere else to turn, we turn to Him. Prayer shouldn't be reserved for an emergency hotline, but if that's the only way for God to get us to pick up the phone and start talking, He'll use it. The disciples saw a different kind of prayer life in Jesus; that's why they asked Him to teach them how to pray. Life lived out of that deep, ongoing communion with the Father is a life worth living. The more we co-operate with the Lord in prayer, the smoother our journey, the better we navigate life's storms and the more heavenly courage and wisdom we have with which to face them.

For prayer and reflection

What's *your* 'reflex prayer?' How is it being fulfilled in your life? Does it need to change so that you can develop a deeper communion daily with the Father?

At home **with God**

'... my prayer rose to you, to your holy temple.' (v.7)

Have you ever been somewhere you thought you'd never find God? Somewhere He just wouldn't fit – too dark or too sinful? I had that feeling in a young offenders' prison; when I visited a former slave fort in Ghana; when I went to a heavy metal concert with my school friends. Yet, in all those dark places, I had a powerful encounter with Jesus and saw that others could find Him there too.

When Solomon dedicated the Temple 200 years earlier, he prayed that God would always hear His servants when they prayed towards it. He knew the Lord couldn't be contained there; the heavens and the earth were too small for Him. But if He'd keep one eye on His Temple, perhaps the prayers of even his wayward people could reach Him there (1 Kings 8:27–30).

Jonah thought God would never stoop so low as to meet him in a fish on the ocean bed; God wouldn't even look at him there (v.4). His theology taught him that God was to be found in His Temple, but his experience showed him that, even at 'the roots of the mountains' (v.6), he could encounter the Lord. He hoped that in spite of his disobedience and his unholy, unlikely surroundings, God might still draw near to him. He wasn't disappointed! The divine encounter caused him to pray in the past tense: 'You ... *brought* my life up from the pit ... my prayer *rose* to You' (vv.6–7). In the belly of a fish, Jonah had a revelation of his God who would one day enter into the womb of a woman. He thought God dwelt only in palaces (palace and temple are the same word in Hebrew), but the Bible states that He made His home in a stable. Jesus came to 'fill all things' so that we could find Him anywhere (Eph. 4:10).

For prayer and reflection

Where do you find it difficult to feel God's presence? Your workplace? Around a particular person? Pray: Lord Jesus, fill that place/relationship and meet me there.

Faith vs fear

Jonah 2:8–10

'Those who cling to worthless idols turn away from God's love ...' (v.8)

Jonah's comparison here is outrageous, it sounds like a sideswipe at the pagan sailors who threw him overboard: 'Those idol-worshippers may have begun to pray to You, Lord, but their devotion won't last. I'm the one who'll keep worshipping you when this is all over!' Considering his position, Jonah was pretty bold to play himself off against the sailors before God!

I remember getting very irritated with a guy in my Hebrew class. He was rude, aggressive and acted thoroughly bored during lessons, like he knew it all already. I was delighted when our Jewish teacher approached him. I couldn't wait for her to take him down a peg or two. But to my amazement, she quietly said 'I'm sorry you don't enjoy my lessons. Perhaps you'd get more out of them if you thought about how you'd put things over if you were me. I believe you're going to make an excellent Hebrew teacher one day!' The graciousness of her attitude touched me. Here was a Jew displaying more of Jesus' character than me, the Christian.

It's easy to assume we're God's favourites, that He sees everything from our perspective and makes allowances for our 'well-intentioned' mistakes. We can write others off as spiritual novices when in fact, Jesus would commend them.

Jonah *did* have one thing in his favour: the sailors prayed to the Lord out of *fear* of His wrath, whereas he knew the Lord's character. He prayed from a place of *faith* that God wanted to save him. The Lord is looking for a relationship with us based on faith, not fear, and in that respect Jonah had it right. 'Without faith it is impossible to please God ...' (Heb. 11:6)!

For prayer and reflection

Where have you been praying to God out of fear more than faith? Pray: Lord, open my eyes to see Your heart for this situation and show me what You want to do in it. Amen.

A God of **second chances**

'Then the word of the LORD came to Jonah a second time …' (v.1)

A man in his eighties once told me 'I had my chance to turn to Jesus as a teenager, but I rejected Him. It's too late for me now!' However old we are, we can all look back on missed opportunities for the Lord.

At university, my friend's brother dived into a shallow river after drinking heavily at his stag do. He broke his neck and the doctors thought it unlikely he'd ever walk again. I sat with my friend as he wept, trying to gather the courage to offer to pray for him and his brother. But I feared he'd feel manipulated, or that his brother wouldn't get healed. So I said nothing. I regretted it for days; the Lord had prompted me to speak up for Him, but I'd ignored Him. Eventually I wrote a card to my friend explaining about the power of prayer and that I was praying for his brother's full healing. I did pray, along with others, and miraculously, a few weeks later his brother was walking again. His doctors were amazed! Months later, my friend acknowledged 'Your God saved my brother from paralysis!'

I'm so glad God gives second chances. I thought I'd missed my opportunity to witness to my friend, but He showed me how to create another one. Jonah was re-commissioned; this time, he obeyed. God could've given up on him, moved on, found someone else to go to Nineveh leaving Jonah to deal with a lifetime of regret, feeling left out of His purposes.

However long it's been, don't stay stuck in regrets! Get up, go back to God's last instruction to you and start to follow it. He's gracious, persevering with His people to get the best out of them; you may find He offers you a second chance too!

For prayer and reflection

Bring any regrets before Jesus now: Lord, thank You that Your death and resurrection makes second chances possible. Give me Your power for a fresh start. Amen.

Wholehearted repentance

'A fast was proclaimed, and all of them, from the greatest to the least, put on sackcloth.' (v.5)

A t our after-school kids' club, two children ran riot and broke some expensive equipment. Both were sent to me by their mums to apologise. The first glowered and spat out 'sorry' through pouting lips. The second threw her arms around me and sobbed 'I'm so, so sorry, please forgive me, I'll pay for it from my pocket money!' Naturally it was much easier to respond graciously to the second apology.

The Ninevites demonstrated holistic repentance: from kings to paupers and even animals, their hearts reached out for God's compassion (v.8). Their souls determined to stop their evil ways (v.9). Their minds changed, as they 'believed' God (v.5). They employed all their strength in fasting, wearing sackcloth and fervent prayer (vv.7–8). They couldn't have made a bigger gesture.

It doesn't always follow that the more extravagant the repentance, the more genuine the apology; in fact, it *can* indicate the opposite. But God is moved when we appeal to Him with our heart, soul, mind and strength engaged. Remember Jesus' response to the woman who broke her jar of perfume over Him, or to Zacchaeus as he repaid what he'd stolen fourfold! Their outward actions were bearing out their inner decisions; this combination allows God room to move powerfully into our lives and energise us with His Holy Spirit so that our repentance leads to a lasting change of character.

Don't let pride, fear, self-consciousness, or even cultural disposition hold you back from expressing yourself wholeheartedly before the Lord; you'll find enormous spiritual breakthrough as you let your inner life with Him show.

For prayer and reflection

Are there any outward actions you need to take to strengthen your heart decisions for the Lord? Do you hold back from openly expressing your heart to Jesus? What stops you?

WEEKEND

Praying Bible prayers

For reflection: Jonah 2:1–10

'In my distress I called to the LORD, and He answered me.' (v.2)

H ave you ever faced something so overwhelming you didn't even know how to begin praying about it? Where Jonah's words failed him, the words of Scripture came through. Most of his prayer is quotes from the Psalms. He refers to at least five different psalms in at least seven places: Psalm 130, the Lord hears a sinner's cry; Psalm 18, God delivers His servant from his enemies; Psalm 116, God saves His servant from death, and so on. Having memorised these words of Scripture, Jonah had plenty of relevant material to draw on in prayer.

Bible prayers help us when we're struggling to pray. We can be comforted that others have been through similar things yet found the Lord faithful. We'll also find the Holy Spirit drawing alongside to encourage us as we speak out the Scriptures – after all, they were His words to start with! And even if we begin with little or no faith at all, God's Word causes faith to rise up in our hearts, for 'faith *comes* from hearing, and hearing by the word of Christ' (Rom. 10:17, NASB).

Optional further reading
See if you can spot the quotes in Jonah's prayer from the following psalms: 18; 31; 42; 116; 130; Roger Forster, *Prayer: Living in the Breath of God* (PUSH publishing, 2007)

The heart of the matter

'Have you any
right to be angry?'
(v.4)

I t's a wonderful feeling to be used by the Lord. Remember the first time you stepped out to serve Him? You prayed for someone and they were blessed, or you shared Jesus with someone and they responded. For a short while I bet you thought you were the most spiritual person on earth, soaring in the heavenlies: lucky God, to have a worker like you in His service ...

It doesn't take long to come back down to earth with a bump! Our church leaders once interviewed a young woman for a youth worker's post reaching out to inner city teenagers. She came across brimming with passion, skills and capability. When asked why she wanted the job, her eyes shone, 'Because I just *love* young people!' She got the job. After two weeks of being threatened and sworn at by the local youths she informed the leaders 'It's not working.' 'But why?' they asked. She responded with passion 'Because I *hate* these young people!'

Serving the Lord is the quickest way for our *own* issues to come to the surface. We think we're offering God our abilities and strengths when really He's taking the opportunity to deal with our failings and weaknesses. For this young lady, her self-sufficiency was challenged; she wonderfully responded and learned how to depend on the Lord, drawing from His endless resources of love for those troubled youths. For Jonah, the pride and anger hidden deep in his heart were exposed as he served the Lord as a prophet. Where Nineveh's repentance had been wholehearted, Jonah's was revealed to be only a change of mind, a change of direction; what he really needed, what God was intent upon, was a change of heart.

**For prayer and
reflection**

Lord, I want to
serve You; I'm
willing for You to
change my heart.
Help me not to
be disheartened
when faced with
my inadequacies,
but to look to You
for grace. Amen.

J-O-Y

'It would be better for me to die than to live.' (v.8)

Jonah reasoned, 'I *deserve* God's forgiveness more than Nineveh because 1. they're wicked murderers, 2. I only made one little mistake, and 3. I'm an Israelite!' A bit like the lady who objected when invited to repent of her sin; she could see why others should, but she'd done nothing that bad; she wasn't perfect, but she was sure the Lord understood. Jonah also thought, 'If God loves me and is *on my side*, how can He possibly also love the Ninevites, my enemies?' Like my friend who struggled to receive mercy at the cross because it also offered forgiveness to her father who'd cruelly mistreated her as a child; it didn't seem fair.

The root of both thought patterns is a wrong comparison between how God treats me versus how God treats others. We've probably all had times where we felt unjustly treated by God; that He didn't defend us enough; that after all the sacrifices we made for Him, He should've sorted things out better for us. These are painful times and they were for Jonah too; to him, death seemed the only relief.

The problem with this thinking is that it has 'me' at the centre. We begin with what *we* deserve, how *we* were mistreated, how things should be for *us*. However, if we put God's goodness at the centre of our thinking, our perspective changes. Before the extremity of His sacrifice, we start to feel grateful that He paid such a price for any sin to be forgiven.

Me-centred thinking will only ever produce sorrow. The old Sunday-school song had it right: '*J-O-Y, J-O-Y, surely this must mean, Jesus first, yourself last and others in between!*'

For prayer and reflection

Put Jesus first in your thoughts today. Remember the good things He's done for you; count your blessings and thank Him; worship His beautiful character at the cross.

Anger and **compassion**

'Should I not be
concerned about
that great city?'
(v.11)

We tend to think of compassion as a
Christian virtue and of anger as sinful. I
tried to explain the sad facts of a church
split to a non-Christian friend, how angry and betrayed
some felt by it, and he commented 'That's not a very
Jesus-like reaction!' He thought a Christian must always
smile and say 'Oh, it doesn't matter, think nothing of it!'
But real relationships run deeper than that.

In this passage, the Lord draws a fascinating
comparison between Jonah's anger over the withered
plant and His own compassion on Nineveh. He'd set up
the situation to kindle Jonah's short temper, using the
fiery, gut-wrenching feelings it produced to show him how
He felt as He looked on the Ninevites and showed them
mercy. For God, the anger and the compassion felt similar;
they were all mixed up together in His act of forgiveness.

The sentiment: 'When you cut love, it bleeds
anger' is ascribed to the writings of C.S. Lewis. When
a loved one hurts us, we find our anger spilling
forth from the damage. It's not premeditated; it's the
inevitable outflow of a broken relationship. Left to
flow unhindered, the anger will drain all life from the
wounded one. But properly checked and treated, it
can heal and love again. Forgiveness is a strange
cocktail of anger and compassion. God's anger at our
unfaithfulness was borne by Christ on the cross. At
the same time, His death was proof of His compassion
towards us; God was willing to bear the force and
damage of that anger within Himself, rather than spend
it upon us. Forgiveness and compassion are never
cheap; there's always a cost within as the anger flowing
from the hurt is overcome.

**For prayer and
reflection**

**Are you struggling
to forgive? Pray:
Lord, thank You
that my pain
and anger can
be swallowed
up at the cross
without doing
more damage.
Help me find Your
forgiveness.**

Intimacy and prophecy

Nahum 1:1–6

'The book of the vision of Nahum the Elkoshite.' (v.1)

Jonah spoke only one sentence to Nineveh; Nahum spoke three chapters. Jonah's prophecy was an oracle; Nahum received a vision. Jonah's book focuses on the prophet's story; Nahum's book reveals nothing about the prophet except where he's from; the focus is his message. Jonah felt the Lord was too loving and merciful; Nahum described Him as wrathful and avenging. Nahum used Jonah's phrase (4:2) but with a twist: 'The Lord is slow to anger *but great in power; the Lord will not leave the guilty unpunished*' (Nahum 1:3, my emphasis). Did they speak for the same God?

The prophets used two distinct modes of prophecy. Jonah gives us insight into God's gracious character, anticipating Christ, because he records his intimate conversations with his Maker. Nahum received a premonition of the fall of Nineveh and tried to put those pictures into words. He saw trembling earth and quaking mountains. The present tense, 'The Lord *is* a jealous and avenging God ...' (v.2, my emphasis) doesn't describe a permanent state of character, but rather interprets the apocalyptic visions he was seeing. The chaos depicts God's hurt and anger, but it doesn't tell the whole story of His feelings and His journey with Nineveh over 150 years.

The word 'prophecy' in verse 1 is literally 'burden' in Hebrew. The vision weighed heavily on Nahum, just as it made God's heart heavy to finally bring judgment on the city He loved to stop their evil. Just as we need Jonah's conversations with God to rightly interpret Nahum's visions, so we need intimacy with the Lord to be an accurate prophet for Him.

For prayer and reflection

In 1 Corinthians 13–14, Paul encourages us to pursue prophecy but put love first. When did you last ask God to reveal His thoughts and intentions to you so that you could communicate them to others?

The blessed **hope**

Nahum 1:7–15

'No more will the wicked invade you; they will be completely destroyed.' (v.15)

A stone dropped into the middle of a pond sends out ripples from the impact right to the edge. That one event can be experienced at many points on the radius of the pond; just so, prophecy ripples throughout human history.

Nahum's prophecy describes events experienced in the seventh century BC by Israel and Nineveh, but it also indicates the ultimate impact of God's future purpose: the second coming of Christ to judge the earth. Nahum's language about Nineveh's end anticipates the final destruction of God's enemies when Jesus comes again: 'trouble will not come a second time ... [the wicked] will be completely destroyed' (vv.9,15).

The film *A Time to Kill* based on John Grisham's novel provoked discussion among my non-Christian friends. In a racially prejudiced town in the Deep South a young black girl is brutally raped by two white men. Her father, fearing they'd be acquitted by a white majority justice system, takes the law into his own hands, shooting the criminals dead. When questioned by the Prosecution, he shouts, 'Yes, they deserved to die and I hope they burn in hell!' At this point, the cinema erupted into applause. Afterwards my friends analysed this desire for retribution as unsophisticated. But anyone who has suffered unjustly or seen the defenceless and innocent abused knows that the human heart cries out for a God who will stand up for the weak and oppressed and bring justice.

Our dark world is riddled with injustice; but we have a 'blessed hope' (Titus 2:13): one day our God will appear again to rescue the downtrodden, destroying the Destroyer forever.

For prayer and reflection

Pray for some innocent people you know of who're suffering today; that they'd be comforted by hope in Jesus' coming to judge the world with righteousness (Psa. 96:13).

WEEKEND

The work of the spirit

For reflection: John 16:7–15

'But when he, the Spirit of truth, comes, he will guide you into all the truth.' (v.13)

The Holy Spirit seems absent from the sad stories of Jonah and Nahum. But we can see hints at His presence and activity. Jonah's name means 'dove', a New Testament symbol of the Spirit. Nahum mentions a whirlwind and flames of fire that bring Pentecost to mind. He also describes a reversal of Isaiah 35 and the Spirit's work to bring fruitfulness (cf. Nahum 1:4).

The Holy Spirit makes the world aware of sin, righteousness and judgment. The Ninevites weren't conscious of their *sin* until Jonah's dove and Nahum's whirlwind arrived. They began to be empowered by God's *righteousness* when they received the dove with repentance. The whirlwind, fire and floods signalled the final *judgment* for Nineveh where their sin and evil would be purged from the world.

With Jesus at the Father's right hand in heaven, we could fear that God has finished His activity on the earth. But the Holy Spirit continues God's work in the world, bringing us consciousness of our sin, the power of His righteousness and the knowledge that Satan, our Accuser, has been condemned.

Optional further reading
Nahum 1:3–6; Isaiah 35; Acts 2

The **true vine**

'The LORD will restore [their] splendour ... though destroyers ... have ruined their vines.' (v.2)

Have you ever seen a drastically pruned vine? It can look like a dead tree stump. It may seem impossible for there ever to be flourishing fruitfulness from it again.

That's how God's people Israel felt in the days of Nineveh's power. They were constantly being stripped and plundered by the Assyrian armies. The vine is a common Old Testament picture of Israel. The Lord, their Vinedresser, was faithful in tending the plant so that it would put down roots, be established and bring forth the fruit of His kingdom: righteousness, peace and joy (Rom. 14:17). But, time after time, His vine turned to other nations for protection and care, ending up inevitably plundered and unfruitful. Yet the Lord loved His vine and continued to protect it from destroyers because one day He planned to bring forth a shoot of purest stock into which all other branches would be grafted.

In John 15:1, Jesus declared: 'I am the *true* vine' (my emphasis). Here at last was the genuine article, what God's people were always meant to be. Now people of every tribe, nation and tongue can draw their life from Him and bear kingdom fruit.

If the Lord's judgments of Nineveh through Nahum seem harsh, it was only to preserve His vine from utter destruction until Jesus could be brought forth. As for Israel, God used Nineveh's ravaging to prune them, so that they'd be quickened to bear the fruit of repentance.

If you feel like a ruined vine, plundered or withered, the Lord can prune you too. His cuts may go deep but they won't be fatal; and any good viticulturist will tell you: the more drastic the pruning, the richer the fruit produced.

Are you aware of dead or unfruitful branches in your life? Abide in Jesus; trust Him where He strips you back; let His tender love and care bring forth fresh fruit.

Against military might

Nahum 2:8–13

'I will burn up
your chariots
in smoke' (v.13)

Israel was in awe of the proud armies of Nineveh, stalking about like lions. They'd asked God to give them a king 400 years before so they could build a power structure like other nations and hold their own in a world of wars and alliances. But God utterly opposed Nineveh's military might as a means of achieving wealth, stability and security: 'I am against you!'

Because of Israel's numerous battles, many criticise the God of the Old Testament for endorsing warfare. Others use them to support military means of bringing in 'God's kingdom'. But remember Gideon's army? They won a battle by blowing trumpets and smashing jars! God prefers His people *not* to fight.

Armies and warfare are part of the world's power structures. Humanly constructed societies cannot survive without them. God made use of them in Old Testament times to achieve His purposes; to interact with His fallen world at all, He had to use the available material in mankind. But when Jesus came, God had a perfectly sinless human being from which to generate a new world order.

My friend was once attacked while working at a youth club in a rough city. As the thug bore down on him, he cried out: 'Stop, in Jesus' name!' His attacker was lifted into the air and thrown six feet backwards. No one had laid a finger on him; such is the power of prayer. Hudson Taylor said: 'The prayer power has never been tried to its full capacity.' Let's not be tempted to fall back on worldly answers to humanity's problems, when God has opened up a new way in Christ who said: 'If [my kingdom] were of this world, my servants would fight' (John 18:36).

For prayer and reflection

Think of a war being waged in the world today and pray for a peaceful resolution. Lord, give us more faith in the power of prayer to effect mighty change in our world.

Against greedy gain

'… all because of … wanton lust … [that] enslaved nations …' (v.4)

The Lord describes the city of Nineveh as a prostitute who enslaves nations; her fall prefigures the destruction of the symbolic city of Babylon, the 'Mother of Prostitutes' (Rev. 17–18). The two cities have many parallels: both are called 'the Great City' (Jonah 4:11; Rev. 17:18); both are connected with rivers, showing their strength to lie in trade routes and commerce (Nahum 3:8–9; Rev. 17:15); both are associated with evil spiritual power (Nahum 3:4; Rev. 18:2).

Babylon is a New Testament symbol of exploitative commerce, a desire for amassing wealth and squandering it on pleasure. Nineveh shared many of Babylon's characteristics. God's reaction to her shows us His disgust with the power of greed fuelled by demonic energy that pervades our world still today: 'I am against you' (Nahum 3:5)!

I once bought a hard-up kid a Mars bar from the youth club tuck shop. As he ripped it open, I half noticed a flash of gold. The next day I saw on TV: 'A gold wrapper Mars bar wins a gold ingot worth £1,000!' My stomach churned: I'd paid for the Mars bar, the prize was rightfully mine. What if the boy threw the wrapper away? What a waste! Should I go back and check the bins? Should I find out if he'd claimed the prize …? A moment later I was ashamed. I hadn't earned that prize; and why should I begrudge it to a little boy whose family needed the money more than me?

We may not easily be able to rid our world economy of greed and exploitation. But we can root it out of our own hearts. Every person deciding to live by different priorities weakens the power of greed at work in our world today.

For prayer and reflection

Lord, show me where greed has a grip on me. Give me steps I can take to be set apart from worldly values of self-advancement. May I use my resources to raise others up.

A house **on the sand**

Nahum 3:10–19

'... strengthen your defences ... repair the brickwork!' (v.14)

During this 'global recession', we've all heard reports of highly paid financiers attempting suicide because their jobs are under threat. They'd poured all their energy into earning themselves a happy life and so felt there was nothing left to live for once that lifestyle was lost.

After a grand description of Nineveh's military prowess, charging cavalry and glittering spears, we find her very weak and vulnerable after all. When trouble came, she found herself imprisoned, alone, her children unprotected, cowardly with flimsy defences, wide open to attack, too weak to fight back; those she once looked to for wisdom and leadership were deposed or abdicating. Perhaps that's how some of those desperate bankers felt. Instead of strengthening defences, Nineveh had multiplied merchants; her soldiers were better equipped to close a deal than to wield a sword.

Fifteen years ago, my bank manager laughed at me for refusing a credit card. I wanted, perhaps idealistically, to follow Paul's example and 'owe nothing to anyone' (Rom. 13:8, NASB). Today many who *apply* for credit will be laughed at. What seemed like such a secure and profitable way of living has proved risky and flawed. We'll never avoid every pitfall; but if we listen to Jesus and do what He says, He promises that our lives will be strong and unshaken, like a house built on rock. Lives lived according to worldly wisdom may seem better situated on the sandy beach, much more conducive to a happy life. But, when the winds blow and the waves slam against that house, it'll fall with a crash.

Invest in spiritual life, not the 'good life', and be rich towards God!

For prayer and reflection

Lord, give me wisdom and discernment in life to make choices that don't just look strong but also prove to be founded in You, sheltered under Your protection. Amen.

Remember your **roots**

Exodus 34:4–21

'So Moses chiselled out two stone tablets like the first ones ...' (v.4)

W e all need reminding where we've come from in our journey with Jesus once in a while. God told Moses to reissue the Ten Commandments and restate His covenant with Israel after their unfaithfulness with the golden calf. Perhaps Nahum had this story in mind not only as he prophesied Nineveh's destruction, but also to remind Israel who they really were. The bulk of Nahum's prophecy is directed at Nineveh; but he addresses three remarks to Israel, a promise (1:12), a command (1:15) and another promise (2:2). Similarly, the Exodus passage is a list of commands sandwiched between covenant promises.

Nahum 1:2–3 reflects the Lord's description of Himself in Exodus 34:5–7,14: jealous, slow to anger, punishing the guilty. Nahum 3:4 uses the same prostitution imagery as Exodus 34:15–16, a warning to God's people not to run after other gods like other nations. Nahum 1:15 echoes Exodus 34:18: God's people were to keep celebrating their festivals, marking God's faithfulness to them, preserving their distinctiveness among the nations. Exodus 34:21 contrasts Nahum 3:16–17: God's people are to rest from labours and not be driven by greed and consumerism like Nineveh.

Other hints at the Exodus in Nahum's prophecy include God's enemies engulfed in a flood (1:8) plus lots of other watery imagery invoking the crossing of the Red Sea, a yoke of slavery broken off Judah (1:13) and the death of the children of God's enemies (3:10).

As Nineveh was judged, God wanted His people to remember their roots, to come out and be separate from ungodly influences; to be different and worthy of their calling.

For prayer and reflection

Remember how you first became a follower of Jesus. How did you express your love and devotion to Him then? Does anything in your relationship with Him need reviving?

WEEKEND

One small step for man

For reflection: John 7:37–52

'Look into it, and you will find that a prophet does not come out of Galilee.' (v.52)

Jonah and Nahum were two of three prophets to Gentile nations: the third was Obadiah to the Edomites. They showed God's heart was for the whole world, not just Israel – a hard truth to find in Old Testament days. When Jesus came, He filled out the revelation they'd sketched for us: God so loved *the world* He gave His only Son that *whoever* believes in Him shall have eternal life (see John 3:16).

But people doubted: prophets don't come from unimportant places like Galilee … they should have studied their prophets more carefully! Jonah was from Gath-hepher, a town in lower Galilee; Capernaum ('Village of Nahum' in Hebrew) was named after Nahum, leading some to suppose it was his birthplace. Both prophets were associated with Galilee, where Jesus' ministry centred. Thus both played a part in convincing people that Jesus, with His radically inclusive theology and questionable origins, really *was* sent from God. Throughout these studies we've seen how Jonah and Nahum point towards God's bigger plan in Christ. May our small steps of obedience afford giant leaps for God's purposes too.

Optional further reading

2 Kings 14:23–25; N.T. Wright, *Scripture and the Authority of God* (New York: Harper One, 2011)

From this place ...

This September, CWR celebrates 25 years of ministry at Waverley Abbey House, Surrey, England. In 1987, CWR's founders and directors – Selwyn Hughes, Trevor Partridge and David Rivett – opened the doors of the refurbished Georgian building, and a bold new vision began to unfold: to equip men and women of conviction to build the Body of Christ and change their communities for good; to impact the Church, the nation and the world.

By God's grace, and with the support of CWR's Partners, many elements of that vision have been achieved. Around 6,000 visitors and students are impacted each year, and millions are reached through Bible-reading resources, with the help of national distributors in 22 nations and translations in 48 languages. The ripple effect from Waverley Abbey House is both humbling and in the truest sense, awesome.

Now, in its twenty-fifth year, Waverley Abbey House is set to become the pivotal hub for some exciting developments. With expectant hearts we thank God for the work He has begun here, and trust Him for the new chapters of His ministry – not least the recent purchase of Pilgrim Hall, an additional conference centre in East Sussex with facilities that will enable us to continue towards the goal of establishing a Christian college of education. We thank you also for your continued interest and support, and ask for your prayers as we move forward.

Perhaps, to mark this significant year, you would like to become a CWR Partner. For more information, contact our Partnership Coordinator, Robin Pickford, on **01252 784707** or visit **www.cwr.org.uk/partners**

Forgiveness

Matthew 6:5–15

'Forgive us
our debts, as we
also have forgiven
our debtors.' (v.12)

For prayer and reflection

Lord, thank You
for Your wonderful
message of
forgiveness.
Please help me
put it into practice,
so allowing
forgiveness to
transform my own
life and that of
others. Amen.

Forgiveness is one of the most important themes in the Bible – but it is also, sadly, one of the most neglected. When we have been wronged, it's only natural to feel angry and hurt. We may long for justice, or even seek to 'get even'.

For those who've been betrayed or abused, or who have watched those close to them suffer, the process of forgiveness can be a long, painful spiritual journey. Reaching a position of forgiveness may take months, years or decades. It may not even be possible in our lifetime, but Christ's example shows us what we should be aiming towards. We'll go on to consider some of these difficult issues later in the month.

For others, it's not the act of forgiveness itself that causes such difficulty, but accepting that they themselves have been forgiven. Maybe you have hurt someone badly or committed some act that goes against the Bible's teaching and, no matter how many times you apologise, the guilt still weighs heavily upon you. If so, there's great news for you! Forgiveness is possible; as Jesus' teaching on prayer shows (v.12), we are instructed to pray for forgiveness.

But, just as we have been forgiven, we also are called to forgive. The Greek word for 'forgive' is *aphiemi*, meaning to 'send away 'or 'let go'. When we forgive, we are willing to let go of our 'right' to resentment, revenge and obsession. We are willing to start again, refusing to let the bitterness of past hurts have a hold on us.

The truth of God's forgiveness is powerful. Understanding it will free us to be the people He created us to be. Will you accept His forgiveness today?

Why **forgive?**

'... if you hold anything against anyone, forgive him, so that your Father in heaven may forgive you your sins.' (v.25)

The word 'forgive' appears about 56 times in the Old and New Testaments, with the word 'forgiven' a further 42 times. Jesus made it one of the key themes of His ministry – exhorting His disciples to forgive (Matt. 18:21–34), and even praying for the forgiveness of those who put Him on the cross (Luke 23:34). Why does forgiveness matter so much? There are many reasons, but let's consider a few.

The first is that forgiveness helps us to heal. It stops us being prisoner to hurt, bitterness and anger. As theologian Lewis Smedes says: 'When we genuinely forgive, we set a prisoner free, and then discover that the prisoner we set free was us.'* The second is that determining to forgive stops the cycle of hatred. When we have been deeply hurt, the temptation to strike back is overwhelming, but doing so simply prolongs the battle. That is why Jesus, on the night He was to be betrayed, urged His disciples: 'Love one another. As I have loved you, so you must love one another' (John 13:34).

The third is that forgiving is essential for our own forgiveness. It is not that God's forgiveness is conditional upon our own behaviour (because everyone is forgiven at the cross, even before they have repented) but simply that we cannot fully accept it whilst we are still living in a state of unresolved bitterness and anger. That is why Jesus preached that we need to be reconciled with our brothers and sisters before we can approach His altar (Matt. 5:23–24). If you are still finding forgiveness difficult, pray to God today that He will open your heart and help the process of healing begin afresh in you.

*Lewis Smedes, *The Art of Forgiving* (Westminster, MD: Ballantine Books Inc, 1997).

For prayer and reflection

Lord, help me to realise that, even when forgiveness seems impossible, nothing is impossible for You. Amen.

How many times?

'Lord, how many times shall I forgive my brother when he sins against me?' (v.21)

ew things have probably been more devastating to the Body of Christ than unforgiveness. To many non-Christians, the Church appears a place of division. Internal arguments about doctrine, worship or the ordination of women can act for many as a barrier to receiving the true teaching of Christ. If Christians can't even agree with one another, they figure, what hope have they of helping the rest of us?

When Peter questioned Jesus on the subject of forgiveness, he was probably hoping for a reiteration of the rabbinical teaching that an offender should be forgiven three times. Instead, Jesus comes up with 'seventy times seven' – a number so huge he might as well have told Peter to forgive an infinite number of times!

He goes on to reiterate the point with a parable illustrating the consequences of unforgiveness. If we do not forgive others then, like the servant in the story, we have no right to demand God's forgiveness in our own lives. It's not that God denies us His fellowship; just that we cannot profess to love Him whilst consciously demonstrating attitudes of resentment (or even hatred) towards our Christian brothers and sisters.

Yes, forgiveness is difficult – sometimes seemingly impossible, even. But the alternative – being out of step with one another, and out of fellowship with the Lord – is far, far worse. Pray for God's healing forgiveness to come into your life today.

For prayer and reflection

Are there differences or divisions in your church today? What could you, personally, do to bring about reconciliation and forgiveness?

Who started it?

Leviticus 19:15–18

'Do not seek revenge or bear a grudge against one of your people, but love your neighbour as yourself.' (v.18)

I clearly remember my first – and only – fight at school. I was aged, maybe, five or six. Having just started school, I was still learning the names of my classmates when a precocious little girl came up and introduced herself. 'Hello,' she said, 'I'm Rebecca.' 'No, you're not!' I answered back, stamping my foot on the classroom floor, 'You're *not* Rebecca. *I* am Rebecca!' A fist-fight quickly ensued. Eventually, the teacher intervened, pulling us apart.

It's often the stupid little things that start disagreements and arguments. My mum remembers, as a child, listening to her parents having a stand-up row – over a box of matches! Sometimes these petty grievances can last for years.

We tend not to think of the Old Testament as having a lot to say about forgiveness but, in fact, the reverse is true. Here, in Leviticus, we see the roots of Jesus' commandment to 'Love your neighbour as yourself' (Luke 10:25–28). However, Jesus took things one step further. According to Him, our neighbour is not just our fellow believer, but anyone we happen to encounter – including our supposed enemy. To illustrate the point, He told the story of the Good Samaritan (see Luke 10:30–37).

Such divinely inspired encounters only take place when we are willing to lose our hatred and sense of injustice and to acknowledge our common humanity, through faith in the One who made us. Usually, when a fight breaks out, the first question to be is asked is: 'Who started it?' Perhaps a more appropriate question to ask might be: 'Who is going to end it?'

For prayer and reflection

Are you perhaps still nursing an age-old grievance or harbouring a prejudice? Ask God to intervene and to help you to see the other person from His point of view.

Forgive **and forget?**

'And he kissed all his brothers and wept over them. Afterwards his brothers talked with him.'(v.15)

We've talked about what forgiveness is. Today, I want concentrate upon what it is not. Forgiveness is not sweeping things under the carpet, excusing the inexcusable, or pretending we have not been hurt. Neither is forgiveness refusing to administer justice. I can forgive someone who hurt me, but that doesn't mean that they should be let off facing the consequences of their actions, particularly if a criminal act has been committed.

Forgiveness does not always mean forgetting, but it means handing the matter over to God, and refusing to let the hurt and bitterness control and dominate our life. We find a good example of this in the story of Joseph (Gen. 45:1–28). Joseph had every reason to be angry with his brothers who, out of hatred, had thrown him into a pit to die then sold him into slavery. In spite of this, he refuses to strike back and ends up becoming reconciled to them.

I'm quite sure that Joseph was never completely able to forget his treatment at the hands of his brothers. I wonder if, looking at them, he was always haunted by memories of that deep, dark pit of hatred. No, he could not forget, but somehow, against all odds, he learned to do something more wonderful. He'd seen the very worst his brothers were capable of and, even though he knew they didn't deserve it, determined to love them anyway. That's how, after the birth of his first son, Joseph was able to say 'God has made me forget all my trouble and all my father's household' (Gen. 41:51). Though his past couldn't be altered, his future could – and he chose to forgive. What God did for Joseph, He can also do for you.

For prayer and reflection

Dear Lord, You know that right now I am finding it impossible to forget the past hurts done to me. Please give me the strength to trust in Your forgiveness.

WEEKEND

'It's not fair!'

For reflection: Luke 15:11–32

*'But we had to celebrate and be glad, because this brother of
yours was dead and is alive again ...' (v.32)*

Whenever I read this parable, I can't help
siding with the elder brother. Why should the
younger brother, who squandered the family
fortune, get all the best treatment when he clearly doesn't
deserve a penny? It just doesn't seem fair!

And that's the point, really. God's grace isn't fair,
because it isn't about what we've done, it's about *who He is*
and *who we are.* If being a parent has taught me anything, it's
that when it comes to your children what matters first is that
you love them. My daughter can have the most monstrous
tantrum or drive me crazy with her messy eating, but when it
comes down to it, I still love her, because she's *her.*

Nothing you can do can make God love you any more
or any less. God wants to love you, not to punish you. No
matter how far you have moved from Him, He longs to
welcome you back. And the same applies to others, even
those who have hurt us very deeply. It's a tough lesson to
learn – but also, potentially, one of the most beautiful.

Optional further reading
The story of the Good Samaritan (Luke 10:30–37)
Lewis Smedes, *The Art of Forgiving: When You Need To Forgive And
Don't Know How* (Westminster, MD: Ballantine Books, 4th edit., 1997)

Barriers to forgiveness

**Colossians
3:12–17**

'Bear with each
another and
forgive whatever
grievances you
may have against
one another.' (v.13)

Although essential for our healing, forgiveness is anything but easy. So, this week, I want us to consider barriers that prevent us forgiving others.

One major difficulty is that often we don't even realise that we're holding onto past hurts and resentment. We think that we've put the matter behind us but, out of the blue, the old, familiar emotions resurface.

Jesus used the metaphor of a fruit tree to describe the spiritual life (Matt. 12:33). A tree may look outwardly pretty and well-nourished but, if its fruit is bitter and inedible, there's clearly something wrong! If, in spite of your efforts, you still feel hopeless, angry and bitter, the chances are that unforgiveness may be lurking.

We may find forgiveness difficult, even impossible, for many reasons. We may need counselling to help us deal with the emotions of hurt or fear, before forgiveness can even begin. Or we may be afraid to let go of our pain and to forgive, for fear of being hurt again. But, until we've learned to forgive, we'll continue to be affected by past hurt. If this is you, let today's passage encourage you. There is a simple weapon every Christian can draw on – love.

By putting on the love of Christ and allowing ourselves to be permanently permeated by His grace, we'll find that gradually the negative emotions of hurt, bitterness and anger start to disappear. This may take time but, by acknowledging our need, we'll have taken the important first step towards healing past hurts and moving forward in forgiveness.

For prayer and reflection

Lord, however long it takes, please bring me to the point where I may say, along with Jesus: 'Father, forgive them'. Amen.

Barriers to forgiveness: **anger**

**Ephesians
4:17–32**

'Do not let the sun
go down while you
are still angry, and
do not give the
devil a foothold.'
(vv.26–27)

Recently I saw a documentary on the Yellowstone National Park. Watching as the camera panned out across the breathtaking mountain vistas and famous Old Faithful geyser, it was easy to see why it's one of the United States' best-loved areas of natural beauty. But then we learned of its deadly secret: this famous beauty spot is built on one of the most powerful volcanoes on earth. About 4 miles beneath the surface is a 40-mile-wide chamber, full of molten rock under incredibly high pressure. Nobody knows exactly when, but sooner or later it will erupt, destroying everything in its wake.

Anger is a bit like that. We can bury it for so long, but sooner or later all those hidden feelings of hatred, bitterness and wounded pride will come bubbling up to the surface – often with devastating results.

We live in a society where the results of unresolved anger are all around us: fragmented communities, broken relationships, domestic violence, murder. Anger demands an outlet. If it doesn't find one then, like the volcano, it can quickly explode into physical violence.

'Never go to bed on an argument' is good advice for any relationship (although wisdom suggests that any serious discussion should not happen when overtired!). By resolving our disputes quickly, they are brought into the open, acknowledged and dealt with before having a chance to grow into huge, festering grudges. It's the biblical equivalent of 'kiss and make up', or the arm of a parent around a child, assuring them that they are still loved, even though they've just been told off for doing wrong. It's a lesson most of us could learn.

For prayer and reflection

Lord, please enable me, with Your help, to exercise self-control and be 'quick to listen, slow to speak and slow to become angry' (James 1:19).

Barriers to forgiveness: **bitterness**

**Hebrews
12:14–15**

'See to it that no
one misses the
grace of God and
that no bitter root
grows up to cause
trouble and defile
many.' (v.15)

I love gardening, but unfortunately I'm not very good at it! My mum, who is a keen gardener, recently came round to help me sort out my tangled wilderness of a backyard. 'The problem with you, Becky,' she told me, 'is that you're not digging deep enough. It's no use simply cutting the heads off the weeds and hoping that they won't grow back. If you want to keep a tidy garden, you've got to tackle things at the roots.'

In this passage, the apostle Paul refers to bitterness as a root – and with good reason. Just like weeds, our deep-down resentments, if left to grow, can threaten to choke and entangle other areas of our lives, making us hardened and cynical. The problem with carrying such bitterness around with us is that it is catching. We don't just hurt ourselves, but also those around us – our friends, our relatives and our future relationships.

Sometimes we may even have outwardly forgiven someone but, like the child in the playground who says 'sorry' through gritted teeth to avoid punishment, the anger and resentment lingers on.

Today's passage tells us that, instead of holding onto past hurts, we are called to 'make every effort to live in peace with all men'. Why? Because we ourselves have been forgiven. As we read: '... I cancelled all that debt of yours ... Shouldn't you have had mercy on your fellow servant just as I had on you?' (Matt. 18:32–33) and 'Forgive as the Lord forgave you' (Col. 3:13).

We can't afford not to forgive – the cost of not forgiving is way too high. Why not go to God right now, and ask Him for the strength to forgive?

**For prayer and
reflection**

**Lord, Your
command to
'make every effort
to live in peace
with all men'
seems almost
impossible!
Please help me to
root out any past
bitterness and
live afresh for You
today. Amen.**

Barriers to forgiveness: **revenge**

A s a child, I was always a big fan of fantasy epics like *The Lord of the Rings* and *Star Wars*. With bated breath, we'd follow our heroes into the most perilous situations, battling against impossible odds, then heave a sigh of relief as we watched them triumph, victorious over their enemies.

In the world of fantasy fiction, enemies are always defeated. In the real world, more often than not, we simply have to learn to live with them. Doing so normally means resisting the dreadful urge to wreak revenge – tempting though this may be.

One of the problems with revenge is that it ultimately transforms us into the very thing we are fighting against. The Bible is quite clear on this – it is not our role to take revenge, but it is up to God to judge. Romans 12:19 counsels: 'Do not take revenge ... but leave room for God's wrath'.

Nevertheless, we should not sit tight and hope for God to wreak vengeance on our behalf! The danger here is that we have simply transferred our own vengeful desires onto God. If we truly desire God's best for people, we will not want to see our enemies punished but saved, as we ourselves have been forgiven by God. That is why Proverbs 24:17 tells us: 'Do not gloat when your enemy falls; when he stumbles, do not let your heart rejoice.'

By handing the matter over to God, we have to accept both His justice and His mercy. We move from the 'tit for tat' of violence and retribution to the 'give and take' of forgiveness.

1 Thessalonians 5:12–24

'Make sure that nobody pays back wrong for wrong, but always try to be kind to each other and to everyone else.' (v.15)

For prayer and reflection

Lord, please forgive me when I am tempted to lash out in vengeance. Help me to trust in Your goodness and mercy, since You are the perfect judge. Amen.

Barriers to forgiveness: **payback time**

1 Peter 3:8–12

'... be compassionate and humble. Do not repay evil with evil or insult with insult, but with blessing ...' (v.9)

Y ou can learn a lot about human nature by looking at the school playground. Before I became a mum, I used to think that human beings were basically co-operative. A couple of afternoons in a mums and toddlers' group, watching little ones battle it out for toys they wanted no one else to have, soon put paid to that!

Sadly, a lot of us remain toddlers in our spiritual lives. We might feel warm and cosy on a Sunday morning when the preacher tells us to love our neighbour as ourselves, and to 'do unto others as you'd have them do to you', but when on Monday morning we discover that the office junior has 'borrowed' our biscuits again out comes the red-eyed toddler monster, wielding a plastic hammer!

In Jesus' time, a favourite quote among the rabbis was based on Exodus 21:24: 'An eye for an eye, a tooth for a tooth' (see also Lev. 24:20, Deut. 19:21). What seems to us draconian was actually originally intended as a lesson in justice, at a time when the severity of punishment often far outweighed that of the original crime. But Jesus takes things one step further. Rather than giving others their 'just deserts', we are to be those who refuse to strike back physically (see Matt. 5:38–39).

When somebody wrongs us, we are to be those who bless, not curse, our enemies. We do this because we inherit something infinitely more precious than a prized biscuit or a stolen rattle. We inherit a blessing which is eternal: 'And the God of all grace, who called you to his eternal glory in Christ ... will himself restore you and make you strong, firm and steadfast' (1 Pet. 5:10). What an amazing promise!

For prayer and reflection

'When we are offended at any man's fault, turn to yourself and study your own failings. Then you will forget your anger ...' (Epictetus – Greek philosopher).

A spirit of reconciliation

For reflection: 2 Corinthians 5:16–20

'All have sinned and fallen short of the glory of God.
The hatred which divides nation from nation,
race from race, class from class,
Father Forgive.'
The covetous desires of people and nations
to possess what is not their own,
Father Forgive
The greed which exploits the work of human hands
and lays waste the earth,
Father Forgive.
Our envy of the welfare and happiness of others,
Father Forgive.
Our indifference to the plight of the imprisoned,
the homeless, the refugee,
Father Forgive.
The lust which dishonours the bodies of men, women and
children,
Father Forgive.
The pride which leads us to trust in ourselves and not in God,
Father Forgive.
Be kind to one another, tender-hearted, forgiving one
another, as God in Christ forgave you.'*

Optional further reading
Proverbs 25:28; Matthew 5:38–48

*From the *Coventry Litany of Reconciliation*, prayed every Mon–Thurs, Sat. at noon in the new
Coventry Cathedral (Fri at noon in the ruins of St Michael's Cathedral, bombed in 1940). See
www.coventrycathedral.org.uk Used with permission.

Anyone for *Coffee with God*?

A military lifestyle can be very different from a civilian one. On the one hand there can be the security and camaraderie of living and working with the same people, while for many it can be a lonely place, especially as a Christian. What's more, six months (the length of most operational tours) can seem a very long time, especially when separated from loved ones. Imagine then, the luxury of a daily chat with a special friend over a cup of coffee – thinking about life, God, and how on earth they relate to the military!

Passionate about encouraging serving women and those left at home, Liesel Parkinson and a group of women from the Armed Forces Christian Union prayed about creating a book to do exactly that. Using the Psalms to provide readings spanning the six-month period and writing from their own experiences of military life, they approached CWR who were delighted to act as publisher for an exciting new title, *Coffee with God*.

An extract from *Coffee with God* based on Psalm 133:

'69.2 cubic metres. What does that mean to you? To me, it is the size of my world – the size permitted by the Army whenever we move. My "world", or all my worldly goods, to be more accurate, has to fit inside a removals lorry. Over the years, I have had to become increasingly inventive about the best way to make everything fit. Sometimes it seems strange to me that, as Christians, we all worship the same God but try to fit Him into our own "church box".

'God loves to see unity amongst Christians and we see real fruit when we can celebrate our unity despite our differences. Today's short psalm highlights God's pleasure when He sees us working together for the good of His kingdom, "for there the LORD bestows his blessing; even life for evermore" (v.3).

Each house we move into challenges my creativity in arranging our possessions in a practical as well as aesthetically-pleasing way. In one house I had to tuck the sitting room rug up behind the sofa to squeeze it in. In another I had to store a favourite bench in the garage. We need this same ingenuity and flexibility when we come to church. Occasionally we might have to put some of our favourite church practices in "the garage" for a time. True unity is not just about an emotion or a religious doctrine, but about putting aside our differences and focusing on the really important things: loving God and loving each other.'

Attractively presented in full colour, but filled with challenging devotionals, *Coffee with God*, although written with those connected to the forces in mind, will speak to women from all walks of life – propelling you on into deeper intimacy with God.

Coffee *with* God

DAILY REFLECTIONS ON THE PSALMS

Written by women in association with The Armed Forces Christian Union

Not final cover

Coffee with God

Compiled by Liesel Parkinson on behalf of the Armed Forces Christian Union

£9.99

Available mid-September 2012

Whose authority?

Matthew 9:1–8

'Which is easier:
to say, "Your sins
are forgiven," or to
say, "Get up and
walk?"' (v.5)

This week, I want to look at some of the teachings of the master of forgiveness – Jesus Himself. Because we're so familiar with the Gospel stories, it's easy to miss just how radical His message was. Today's passage is a good example of this.

The paralysed man must have been totally desperate. Perhaps he'd already tried and failed to get to the Temple, the traditional place to ask for healing. So he decided to approach Jesus, a known miracle-worker, enlisting the help of his friends to get him there.

I wonder what he expected in return? Perhaps to have Jesus lay hands on him? Instead, Jesus responds with: 'Take heart, son; your sins are forgiven' (v.2). This was shocking to the audience on many levels. For starters, the man had sought not forgiveness, but physical healing. But Jesus, seeing his faith, knew that he needed to be healed completely, body and soul. Even more radically, Jesus was offering complete forgiveness of his sins – something those listening believed only God could do (see Lev. 4:26, Psa. 32). Who did Jesus think He was, to take on the role of God?

With our knowledge, in hindsight, of His crucifixion and resurrection, we know exactly who Jesus was – the only Son of the Living God, who died for the sins of mankind, that all might be forgiven and reconciled to God.

Only when we acknowledge our own sinful state and recognise Jesus' awesome power to heal – physically, emotionally and spiritually – can we move on to a new place of faith. The paralysed man knew this – and was wise enough to enlist the help of his friends to bring him to Jesus. Will you do the same?

For prayer and reflection

Have you ever reached a point where you felt 'paralysed' in your spiritual journey? Do you have friends of faith, to call when the going gets tough?

Love **your enemies**

'Love your enemies, do good to those who hate you, bless those who curse you, pray for those who ill-treat you.' (v.27–28)

Love your enemies – three short words, but possibly the three hardest words to put into practice in the whole of the English language! A few years ago, I was humiliated and let down very badly by a former work colleague whom I had previously trusted and respected. Did I feel like loving her? Absolutely not! What I longed for, more than anything, was to see her downfall; to 'get even' in some way. And yet, that is not the way of Jesus.

Instead, Jesus tells us that we should love our enemies, bless them and pray for them. Why? Because hatred is ultimately destructive, not just to the person we hate, but also to the person doing the hating. It keeps us trapped in a place of bitterness and prevents us receiving all God has for us.

A story is told of the great artist Leonardo da Vinci. Shortly before starting work on *The Last Supper*, he had a terrible falling out with a fellow artist. When da Vinci painted the face of Judas, he took delight in modelling it on that of his enemy. Then he came to paint the face of Jesus. No matter how hard he tried, it would not go right. Finally, he realised that he couldn't paint the face of Jesus as long as Judas had the face of his enemy. Only after being reconciled with his enemy and repainting the face of Judas was he able to paint the face of Jesus and complete his masterpiece.

Are you trying to paint the face of Jesus in your own life, whilst still holding onto past resentments? If this is you today, ask God to help you, by His grace, to move from a place of hatred and bitterness to one of healing and love.

For prayer and reflection

Do good ... bless ... pray. What practical actions can you take this week to fulfil Jesus' commandments to love your enemy?

Pray for **your persecutors**

'Bless those who curse you, pray for those who mistreat you.' (v.28)

It's funny how, sometimes, our words can come back to haunt us. A few days after writing yesterday's passage, news came through that a prominent terrorist leader had been captured and killed. Almost immediately, the internet and airwaves were filled with messages from people celebrating his demise.

His death, and people's reactions to it, raise some important, and awkward, questions. Is anyone simply too bad – too evil – to warrant God's forgiveness?

The Bible is clear in its hatred of evil and cruelty. Proverbs 8:13 declares: 'To fear the LORD is to hate evil …'; Amos 5:15 demands: 'Hate evil, love good'; and Isaiah 5:20 warns: 'Woe to those that call evil good, and good evil …'.

Yet, the Bible is equally clear that we should not celebrate the demise of our enemies: 'Do not gloat when your enemy falls; when he stumbles, do not let your heart rejoice …' (Prov. 24:17).

We are right to hate any evil acts that have been committed; we are also right to expect justice. But we must not delight in the suffering of another human being: 'Do I take any pleasure in the death of the wicked? declares the Sovereign LORD. Rather, am I not pleased when they turn from their ways and live?' (Ezek. 18:23).

If I'm absolutely honest, I find it quite impossible to like my enemies – let alone to love them! Only by trusting in God, and His perfect justice, can we learn to place the things that hurt us most in the hands of His Son, who prayed on the cross: 'Father, forgive them, for they do not know what they are doing' (Luke 23:34).

For prayer and reflection

Lord, help me to take seriously Your command to love my enemy. Amen.

Turn the **other cheek**

'Do not resist an evil person. If someone strikes you on the right cheek, turn to him the other also.'
(v.39)

When someone hits us, often our first response is to want to strike back. It's only natural to want to inflict pain on the person who has caused us pain. Jesus, however, counsels a different kind of response.

To properly understand this passage, we need to consider its historical context. According to biblical scholar Walter Wink*, in Jesus' time a slap to the right cheek with the back of the hand was probably the sort of punishment administered to lower-class citizens (slaves and servants) by their masters. By offering the left cheek as well as the right, it's a way of refusing this sort of treatment. In effect, it says: 'Look at me; I deserve equal treatment. If you are going to punish me, then at least have the decency to treat me like a human being.' In many ways, it's a lesson in assertiveness over aggression.

Instead of simply accepting aggression, Jesus invites us to show our inner strength by refusing to retaliate violently. The American Civil Rights campaigner Martin Luther King was a good example of this kind of 'non-violent resistance'. Speaking from his prison cell, he wrote the following, now-famous words: 'Somehow we must be able to stand up before our most bitter opponents and say: "We shall match your capacity to inflict suffering by our capacity to endure suffering. We will meet your physical force with soul force. Do to us what you will and we will still love you."'

Love is the only force capable of transforming an enemy into a friend. Hate destroys, but love alone transforms. Ask God to place His love in your heart afresh today.

*Walter Wink, *Jesus and Nonviolence: A Third Way* (Nashville: Abingdon Press, 2003).

For prayer and reflection

Are you facing aggression or opposition today? Ask God to show you how He would have you respond with love, rather than anger.

Doormats ... **or doorways?**

Matthew 5:38–42

'Do not resist an evil person. If someone strikes you on the right cheek, turn to him the other also.' (v.39)

As we saw yesterday Jesus' commandment to 'turn the other cheek' was not an invitation to do nothing about violence or injustice. The danger of applying 'turn the other cheek' to every situation is that we risk turning ourselves into willing victims – particularly in areas like domestic abuse, where those facing abuse may feel it's somehow more 'Christian' to patiently endure suffering than to speak up and end it.*

This is clearly not God's desire for us. In a marriage context, the Bible clearly says we are to treat one another with mutual love and respect. 'Husbands, love your wives and do not be harsh with them' (Col. 3:19; 1 Pet. 3:7–9). Abuse, particularly in the context of a supposedly loving relationship, is contrary to God's plans for us and, as such, should not be tolerated. However, in any context, striking back, either physically or verbally, is rarely useful. 'Turn the other cheek' means reasserting your (and others') right to dignity, not becoming a doormat.

A doormat is designed to be trampled upon. But Jesus was never a doormat! He upset the Temple money-changers and challenged the religious authorities (Mark 11:15–19; Matt. 3:7). Yet at the cross He remained obedient to God's purposes. We are not intended to be 'doormats' – far from it. Instead, we are doorways, through which Christ's love and healing power can flow. Ask God to send you some of His healing power today.

For prayer and reflection

Are you facing a challenging situation, at home or at work? Ask God to show you the right way forward to retain your own dignity, whilst avoiding unhelpful confrontation.

*If you are suffering violence in an abusive relationship, be aware that repeated forgiveness with no other action will allow the abuse to continue. Speak to someone you trust, and together work out a way to either remove yourself from the situation or facilitate a way to stop the abuse.

Organise a breakfast party!

It's a fantastic way to start the weekend, says Angi Pollard

Since becoming a Christian, I've always valued being part of a small group. Over the years, I have met with friends to study the Bible, chat, share our concerns and pray for each other – not necessarily in that order! My husband and I have attended a variety of groups: small (just four of us) to large (over twenty); couples and singles; varying in age from 18 to 80. It has been great fun and a valuable way of growing in prayer and increasing my knowledge of the Bible.

I'm inspired by Hebrews 10:25: 'Let us not give up meeting together, as some are in the habit of doing, but let us encourage one another ...' or, as *The Message* puts it: 'Let's see how inventive we can be in encouraging love ...'

There is nothing that energises me

as much as meeting with like-minded friends round the table, with even the simplest of meals, talking and living with Jesus. I just love 'God-talk'. Whole-hearted, open-hearted, tender-hearted discussion about what it means to be a friend of Jesus.

In the last couple of years, though, I've felt the need to meet with other women. I've also been concerned about women who work outside the home and come to church on their own. It's much harder for them to attend a small group which meets in the evenings and I looked for ways to encourage them.

Occasionally, one or other of the local churches would put on a women's event, with food and a speaker. Still, I wanted more: the events were fun and inspiring, but there wasn't a lot of opportunity to share on a more personal level. So, a couple of years ago, I put out an invitation to women in the church who were working outside the home. With some trepidation –

not knowing how many would come – I invited them to breakfast at my house.

I was worried that too few would come – or too many – but God knew. Around a dozen women turned up. We drank coffee, ate croissants, laughed and chatted. I shared a few thoughts on the challenges of being a Christian out in the workplace, finding others eager to chip in with their own experiences. The next month, I held another breakfast, focusing on a different theme. Then another. And another.

From that initial meeting, we now meet regularly. Although I send out email reminders to over twenty women, numbers vary from six to twelve – always just right. Small enough for intimacy, large enough that shyer women are not forced into discussion. I always marvel at how God brings particular women together, as conversations develop and we find issues in common.

The pattern for the breakfast is simple. Once a month, I get up at 'work time' on a Saturday. I lay the table with a pretty tablecloth, china, a few flowers, cutlery and serviettes. I serve croissants or home-made fruit bread or buns, and I arrange some cut up fruit on a platter.

Women arrive punctually at 9 o'clock, helping themselves to tea, coffee or juice before moving to sit round the table. By 9.15 we are all eating, sharing how our month has gone since we last met. Sometimes we start to discuss the topic quite spontaneously – for example, when the subject was 'stress'! In any case, as we finish eating, I start to talk about whatever has been on my mind recently. It might be a topic, a particular Bible passage or character, or an aspect of Christian life – for example, the type of Christian music I might be listening to on my iPod and how it has affected me. I pray beforehand that the topic will be what God wants.

I am always amazed at how easy it all is. Although giving the house a quick vacuuming on a Friday night and getting up early on a Saturday morning might not sound like a very good idea after a long week, I am invariably refreshed and invigorated by midday on Saturday. Taking the time out for a leisurely breakfast in the company of friends – old and new – is a real break and sets me up for the rest of the weekend. It has been very satisfying to draw in women from many backgrounds: those who attend church sporadically and tend to be uninvolved; even those who rarely attend a church service but come regularly to breakfast.

We all have very busy lives and work full-time outside the home, so this is a little oasis for us as we meet for a couple of hours, sharing our struggles as we work out our salvation in our workplaces. We talk about serving Jesus through serving our colleagues; about prayer; about witness; about being real. We've discussed all manner of topics from talking about how appearance matters to sharing our faith with our colleagues. It amazes me that so often the topic under discussion has been relevant for many of us that week: we see God most definitely at work in our lives!

Every time, in the run-up during the week, I wonder if it is worth it. Discouragement launches a strong attack on my thoughts ... Then there is the uncertainty of knowing who – or how many – are coming. People often don't tell me until the last minute, sometimes not at all ... But, it's worth it. The effort of opening up my home is incredibly satisfying. Just do it!

This article first appeared in full in *Woman Alive*, (September, 2011) Britain's only Christian magazine specifically for women. Used with permission.

womanalive

THE MAGAZINE FOR TODAY'S CHRISTIAN WOMAN

Subscribe by: Email: subs@cpo.org.uk | Tel: 01903 604307 | www.womanalive.co.uk

WEEKEND

The golden rule

For meditation: Luke 6:30–36

'Do to others as you would have them do to you.' (v.31)

What values do you live by? Some people may live by the motto: 'Might is right'. For others, it is: 'Do it to others before they can do it to you'. Or again, it might be: 'He who has gold makes the rules', and so these people seek wealth above all else.

Jesus' commandment is different. Instead of devoting our lives to furthering our own ambitions, we are to seek the good of others – even of those who hurt or persecute us.

We do this because we have been forgiven. None of us can keep God's commandments perfectly. The prophet Ezekiel says, 'The soul who sins is the one who will die' (Ezek.18:4; cf. Rom. 1:28–32). Paul also states 'the wages of sin is death' (Rom. 6:23). Yet, even though we could not win His favour, God has given us an amazing free gift – that of eternal life through His Son, Jesus Christ (Rom. 6:23).

Love is the most precious gift we can offer. Let's make it our rule to show God's love to others today.

What spiritual values do you live by? How do these conflict with the values and philosophies of the world? How does God want you to live?

Optional further reading

Forgiveness and repentance: Luke 17:3–4

Paula Huston, *Forgiveness: Following Jesus into Radical Loving* (Mass: Paraclete Press, 2009)

Looking **inward**

W e've focused so far on forgiving others, but this week I want to consider another aspect of forgiveness – that of forgiving ourselves.

It may be that you are a Christian but you have committed an act which is so bad that you fear God cannot forgive you. Or perhaps you are not yet a Christian but are afraid of becoming one – for fear that God will not accept you, as a sinner?

Alternatively, you may be wondering why a discussion on being forgiven should really involve you. You are basically a good person and, apart from one or two minor misdemeanours, you do not really have anything to be ashamed of. Well, if that's the case, here's some news: you are just as much in need of forgiveness as anyone else! To illustrate that point, Jesus told the parable of 'the Pharisee and the Tax Collector'. One acknowledged his sin, fell to his knees and begged God's forgiveness. The other felt himself to be above such things, considering himself righteous. Instead of choosing the proud, law-abiding religious leader, God favours the one who, though sinful, is humble enough to admit it and seek help and forgiveness.

If, today, you are still struggling to forgive somebody who has wronged you, perhaps it is time to look inward instead. What sort of person do you see? A cold, proud Pharisee, or a sinful, God-dependent tax collector? It's only when we are truly honest about ourselves and our fallen nature that we can realise the futility of judging others. In God's eyes we are all the same – all sinful, all fallen. And yet, in spite of this, He loves each one of us and longs to welcome us home.

Luke 18:9–14

'For everyone who exalts himself will be humbled, and he who humbles himself will be exalted.' (v.14)

For prayer and reflection

The Pharisee went away from his prayer experience empty. The tax collector went away filled with God's gracious forgiveness. Which one are you going to be?

Paid in full!

Colossians
2:9–15

'He erased the
certificate of
debt, with its
obligations, that
was against us
and opposed to
us ...' (v.14, HCSV)

**For prayer and
reflection**

**Are you still
struggling
with an area of
unforgiveness in
your life? Picture
yourself handing
over the matter to
Jesus, and seeing
Him placing it on
the spike marked
'Dealt with'.**

Like most people, I hate getting into debt and always endeavour to pay everything off as soon as possible, before interest has a chance to accumulate. Whenever I get my credit card bill at the end of the month, I must admit to getting a little nervous. How much debt will I have accumulated this time? Will I earn enough to pay it back?

But what about our spiritual debts – those things we can't put a price on? Stop for a moment and think about everything you've done recently that would have dishonoured God – lying, cheating, swearing, gossiping, bad-mouthing others, having sinful thoughts. The Bible tells us what we owe because of this debt: 'For the wages of sin is death ...' (Rom. 6:23).

But here's the good news: through Christ's death on the cross, our debt has been paid – in full! That is how Paul, a former persecutor who watched and approved as the apostle Stephen was stoned to death, can confidently claim: 'He erased the certificate of debt, with its obligations, that was against us and opposed to us, and has taken it out of the way by nailing it to the cross' (Col. 2:14).

An office I once worked in had a very old-fashioned way of processing payments. Outstanding invoices were placed in a metal in-tray. Once paid, they were 'spiked' – placed on an upturned nail, as a sign to everyone that they had now been fully dealt with.

That's how it is with us. All the debts we owe to God, past sins and future temptations, have been nailed to the cross through Jesus' death and resurrection. Our debts truly have been 'Paid in full'!

NOV/DEC 2012

November

THE HEART OF ISAIAH

LIZ HANSFORD

December

DAVID: THE SHEPHERD KING

CATHY MADAVAN

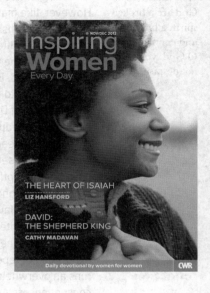

In **November**, Liz Hansford explores Isaiah's message to the nation of Judah, challenging us to *remember* God: who He is, what He has done and what He is yet to do.

In **December**, Cathy Madavan examines the life of David, admonishing us to live authentically, and ultimately find hope in Christ, *our* Shepherd King, this Christmas season.

Obtain your copy from CWR, Christian bookshops or your National Distributor. If you would like to take out a subscription, see the order form at the back of these notes.

Also available as ebook/esubscription

A pleasing **sacrifice**

Psalm 51

'The sacrifices of God are a broken spirit; a broken and contrite heart, O God, you will not despise.' (v.17)

I f ever any man were in need of God's forgiveness, it was King David. Anointed by God to become king of Israel, he had everything going for him. However, like many powerful men, he wanted more. He desired Bathsheba, another man's wife. After committing adultery, King David sent Bathsheba's husband into the front line of battle, knowing that he would be killed. But the consequences of David's sin proved harder to cover up.

The result of David's illicit sexual affair was, as in every case of adultery, catastrophic! In King David's case it was to lead to murder, deception, rape and even civil war (see 2 Sam.11–19). At this stage, it must have been tempting to assume that all was lost; that David was no longer fit to be king, and that God had withdrawn His favour. Instead, David did the sensible thing. He repented.

Psalm 51 is the result – and what a beautiful expression of repentance it is! Throughout the psalm runs an overwhelming consciousness of sin and of its consequences: 'Against you, you only, have I sinned, and done what is evil in your sight, so that you are ... justified when you judge' (v.4). Yet David longs for a time when his brokenness will be restored, his soul washed 'whiter than snow' (v.7) and his joy in the Lord will return.

This psalm is a great encouragement to those who believe that their sins are too great to be forgiven. If God could forgive David so powerfully, then He can forgive us too. We need to learn from David's example, to acknowledge our sin and beg for God's merciful forgiveness. Then, and only then, can God come in and 'make us new'. Try it today and see.

For prayer and reflection

Lord, I'm sorry for the times I've let my own pride get in the way of doing things Your way. Help me to learn from my past mistakes and put You back at the centre of my life. Amen.

Made **new**

Hebrews 10:1–18

Are you perfect? Most of us, if we're honest, will have to admit that we are very far from perfect! We all do, say and think things we know we shouldn't. Saint Paul admitted this when he said: 'I do not understand what I do. For what I want to do I do not do, but what I hate I do' (Rom. 7:15). If even a saint couldn't get it right, what hope is there for the rest of us?

I grew up near Axminster in Devon, a place famous for its carpets. There's a local story that every carpet has an imperfection intentionally woven into it, as a reminder that nobody is perfect apart from God. I'm not sure of the truth of that, but it's an apt illustration for human nature. No matter how beautiful we may look on the outside, all of us have imperfections, little flaws we'd rather keep hidden from the outside world.

In his letter to the Hebrews, however, the writer assures us that we can all be perfect. How so? Because we have been 'made perfect forever' (v.14) by Christ's sacrifice. Before Jesus, the Jews relied on ritual sacrifice to keep themselves right with God. At the centre of this was the Sacrifice of Atonement, an annual offering of two animals 'without mark or blemish' (see Lev. 16), to attain forgiveness for the coming year.

But whereas these sacrifices offered temporary forgiveness, Jesus' death accomplished something nothing else could. By making Himself 'a willing sacrifice' He was able to wipe out our guilt and punishment once and for all – offering 'for all time one sacrifice for sins' (Heb.10:12).

> '... by one sacrifice he has made perfect forever those who are being made holy.'
> (v.14)

For prayer and reflection

We may be full of blemishes and imperfections but, through Christ, we have been made perfect – yes, perfect – in God's eyes! Praise God!

The **X-Factor**

Romans 8:1–12

'Therefore, there is now no condemnation for those who are in Christ Jesus ...' (v.1)

O ne of my guilty pleasures recently has been sitting in front of the television watching ITV's talent show, *The X-Factor*. I laughed and cried as a series of 'hopefuls' paraded before the judges, each of them desperate to convince them that they were good enough to go through to the next round.

Sometimes, I think people imagine the kingdom of heaven to be a little like this. We talk a lot about grace and forgiveness, but in our heads we're still secretly dreading the sound of the Judge's buzzer and the words: 'I'm sorry ... but it's a no from me.'

The Bible tells a different story. According to this beautiful passage from Paul's letter to the Romans, there is no condemnation for those who belong to Christ Jesus – none whatsoever! Paul, a strict Jew, had spent all his life trying to adhere to the Law set out by Moses in the Old Testament. But no matter how hard he tried, he always felt he couldn't measure up.

Perhaps some of us can identify with this? We're like the boy who came running home from school to tell his father he'd gained an A in all his exams, bar one. His father simply frowned, pointed to the subject for which he gained a B, and said, 'What went wrong in this one?'

Compared to God, we will never be good enough but, when we put our faith in Jesus, God sees us through 'Christ-tinted spectacles'. We have our own X-Factor – the X of the cross – and through faith in Him who died for us, we never need fear being told 'You're not good enough'. There is no condemnation for those who are in Christ Jesus. Praise God!

For prayer and reflection

'No condemnation now I dread; Jesus, and all in Him, is mine; Alive in Him, my living Head, and clothed in righteousness divine. Bold I approach the eternal throne, and claim the crown, through Christ my own.' (Charles Wesley)

WEEKEND

Tetelestai – It is finished!

For reflection: John 19:28–30

*'When he had received the drink, Jesus said, "It is finished."
With that, he bowed his head and gave up his spirit.' (v.30)*

'It is finished' are the last words of Jesus before He died. Is Christ giving up? Is this a cry of defeat? Or of victory? In its original Greek, the word for 'it is finished', *tetelestai*, has several meanings. For the priests, it was the equivalent of the Hebrew word spoken by the high priest when he presented a sacrificial lamb on the Day of Atonement. The lamb had to be without blemish, in order to attain temporary forgiveness for the people's sin. The meaning of the high priest's words was: 'Your offering is accepted; it is perfect.'

In a secular sense, the word *tetelestai* was used in the business world to signify the full payment of a debt. When the debt was paid, the parchment was stamped with the word *'tetelestai'*, meaning 'paid in full'. Through His death, offering Himself as a lamb without blemish, Christ presents Himself as the perfect sacrifice, cancelling our sins – for all time. Jesus paid a debt we could never pay, by offering us a gift we could not earn. Praise God – It's been 'paid in full'!

Optional further reading

www.theforgivenessproject.com; R.T. Kendall, *Total Forgiveness: Achieving God's Greatest Challenge* (London: Hodder & Stoughton; 2nd edit., 2003); Jay E. Adams, *From Forgiven to Forgiving: Learning to Forgive One Another God's Way* (Calvary Press, Div. Of Grace Reformed Baptist Church, 2007).

Father, **forgive**

Luke 23:32–44

'Jesus said,
"Father, forgive
them, for they do
not know what
they are doing."'
(v.34)

I remember, as a new Christian, being given a tract entitled: 'Are you Saved?' by a well-meaning member of my church. It listed those groups within society – evangelical Christians, church preachers (but only the *right* sorts of church preachers) – the writer considered to have been 'saved', and all those groups (pretty much everyone else) who had not. After reading it carefully, I filed it in the bin.

Whenever I read this passage, I'm tempted to think about that tract. You see, the thing is, we have a tendency to narrow God's grace to fit our own perspectives, assuming that He is into 'in' groups and 'out' groups just as much as we are, when actually the reverse is true.

If, as I hope and believe I will, I get to heaven, I don't think it will be a cosy place full of people just like me – it will be diverse, and confusing, and wonderful, a melting-pot of languages and creeds and cultures, but we won't care, because we'll all be children of God.

Jesus didn't restrict His forgiveness to those He felt had earned it. Here, on the cross, at a time of the most unimaginable physical and spiritual torment, He calls out to God, not to save Him – but to save those who put Him there.

If we feel uneasy reading that, perhaps it's because we can only too easily imagine ourselves also, at the foot of the cross, joining the mockers and the scoffers. Each of us, in our own way, has rejected Jesus, ignoring His commandments, neglecting the Scriptures, and going about our daily lives as if we don't need Him – and yet He forgives us. Time and time again.

For prayer and reflection

Dear Lord, I thank You that, no matter how many times I fail, You are still willing to let me call You my Saviour. Amen.

'We shall **overcome**'

Romans 12:17–21

'Do not be overcome by evil, but overcome evil with good.' (v.21)

Rev. John Mosey lost his 19-year-old daughter, Helga, in the Lockerbie bombing of Pan Am Flight 103, in 1988. From the beginning, he decided to forgive. Speaking shortly after his daughter's death, he said: 'I saw that if we seek revenge against our enemies we reduce ourselves to their level and make ourselves no better than the terrorists ... our anger must be directed, not against the small fry who plant bombs, but against the arch-terrorist, the force behind all the world's evils, Satan himself.

'But how could I strike back against such a one? My mind went to Paul's Letter to the Romans 12:21: "Do not be overcome by evil, but overcome evil with good."'

Taking this passage as their creed, John and his wife, Lisa, set up the Helga Mosey Memorial Trust. Through it, they have opened homes in India and the Philippines for abandoned and abused children, saving the lives of many. As John himself says: 'What better way of striking back at evil can there be than to bless some of its saddest victims?'*

When we've been hurt or wronged, the temptation is to lash out in anger. But the Bible counsels the opposite approach. It doesn't have to be dramatic – one lovely Christian lady I know used to bring cakes into work every time the boss had annoyed her. The greater the insult, the better the cakes! Such an approach has two effects. It takes the wind out of the sails of our opponent, by placing us back in control. More importantly, perhaps, such a gracious, loving response stops the cycle of violence and anger dead in its tracks, and replaces it with a new cycle – that of Love.

*Used with permission. See also www.e-n.org.uk/p-4873-Can-we-forgive-terrorists.htm

For prayer and reflection

Are you facing an area of conflict today? Ask God how you can respond by turning a situation of evil into a situation of good.

Micah 7:18–19

'You will again have compassion on us; you will tread our sins underfoot and hurl all our iniquities into the depths of the sea.' (v.19)

'No fishing **allowed!**'

As we come to the end of our month considering forgiveness together, I want to end on a note of reassurance. In this wonderful passage from the Old Testament prophet Micah comes the promise of God's total forgiveness. No matter what we have done in the past, if we truly repent of our sins and ask for God's forgiveness, He will grant it. Not only that, but His forgiveness is complete – so much so that it is as if all our sins and iniquities have been cast to the bottom of the ocean!

What goes for us also goes for others. Too often, though we say we have forgiven others, we find ourselves 'going fishing' for their sins. But with God there are no such bitter recriminations. He forgives completely. He purifies from all unrighteousness (1 John 1:9).

The Dutch Christian Corrie ten Boom was held at the notorious Ravensbrück concentration camp during the Second World War, after her entire family was arrested for sheltering Jews from the Nazis. Despite the atrocities she witnessed, including the death of her beloved sister Betsie, she never lost her faith – or her capacity to forgive. In her book *Tramp for the Lord*, Corrie describes how she came from Holland to defeated Germany in 1946, spreading the message that God forgives: 'It was the truth they needed most to hear in that bitter, bombed-out land, and I gave them my favourite mental picture. 'When we confess our sins,' I said, 'God casts them into the deepest ocean, gone forever ... then places a sign out there that says 'No Fishing Allowed!'*

For prayer and reflection

Lord, I'm sorry for all the times when I've seemed to be fishing around for my own sins or those of others. Help me to learn from Your example of total forgiveness. Amen.

*Corrie ten Boom, *Tramp For The Lord* (London: Hodder & Stoughton, new edit., April 2005) p.55.

ORDER FORM

5 EASY WAYS TO ORDER:

1. Phone in your credit card order: **01252 784710** (Mon–Fri, 9.30am–5pm)
2. Visit our Online Store at **www.cwr.org.uk/store**
3. Send this form together with your payment to:
   CWR, Waverley Abbey House, Waverley Lane, Farnham, Surrey GU9 8EP
4. Visit a Christian bookshop
5. For Australia and New Zealand visit KI Entertainment at **www.cwr4u.net.au**

For a list of our National Distributors, who supply countries outside the UK, visit www.cwr.org.uk/distributors

YOUR DETAILS (REQUIRED FOR ORDERS AND DONATIONS)

Name:

CWR ID No. (if known):

Home Address:

Postcode:

Telephone No. (for queries):

Email:

PUBLICATIONS

TITLE	QTY	PRICE	TOTAL
		Total publications	

All CWR adult Bible-reading notes are also available in ebook and email subscription format.
Visit www.cwr.org.uk for further information.

UK p&p: up to £24.99 = **£2.99**; £25.00 and over = **FREE**

Elsewhere p&p: up to £10 = **£4.95**; £10.01 – £50 = **£6.95**; £50.01 – £99.99 = **£10**; £100 and over = **£30**

Please allow 14 days for delivery	Total publications and p&p **A**	

SUBSCRIPTIONS* (NON DIRECT DEBIT)

SUBSCRIPTIONS* (NON DIRECT DEBIT)	QTY	PRICE (INCLUDING P&P)			TOTAL
		UK	Europe	Elsewhere	
Every Day with Jesus (1yr, 6 issues)		£15.50	£19.25	Please contact nearest National Distributor or CWR direct	
Large Print *Every Day with Jesus* (1yr, 6 issues)		£15.50	£19.25		
Inspiring Women Every Day (1yr, 6 issues)		£15.50	£19.25		
Life Every Day (Jeff Lucas) (1yr, 6 issues)		£15.50	£19.25		
Cover to Cover Every Day (1yr, 6 issues)		£15.50	£19.25		
Mettle: 14–18s (1yr, 3 issues)		£13.80	£15.90		
YP's: 11–15s (1yr, 6 issues)		£15.50	£19.25		
Topz: 7–11s (1yr, 6 issues)		£15.50	£19.25		
Total Subscriptions (Subscription prices already include postage and packing) **B**					

Please circle which bimonthly issue you would like your subscription to commence from:

JAN/FEB MAR/APR MAY/JUN JUL/AUG SEP/OCT NOV/DEC

* Only use this section for subscriptions paid for by credit/debit card or
cheque. For Direct Debit subscriptions see overleaf.

CONTINUED OVERLEAF >>

PAYMENT DETAILS

☐ I enclose a cheque/PO made payable to CWR for the amount of: £ _____

☐ Please charge my credit/debit card.

Cardholder's name (in BLOCK CAPITALS) _____

Card No. ☐☐☐☐ ☐☐☐☐ ☐☐☐☐ ☐☐☐☐ ☐☐☐☐

Expires end ☐☐ ☐☐

Security Code ☐☐☐

GIFT TO CWR

☐ Please send me an acknowledgement of my gift **C** _____

GIFT AID (YOUR HOME ADDRESS REQUIRED, SEE OVERLEAF)

giftaid it

I am a UK taxpayer and want CWR to reclaim the tax on all my donations for the four years prior to this year **and on** all donations I make from the date of this Gift Aid declaration until further notice.*

Taxpayer's Full Name (PLEASE USE BLOCK CAPITALS) _____

Signature _____ Date _____

*I understand I must pay an amount of Income/Capital Gains Tax at least equal to the tax the charity reclaims in the tax year.

GRAND TOTAL (Total of A, B, & C) _____

SUBSCRIPTIONS BY DIRECT DEBIT (UK BANK ACCOUNT HOLDERS ONLY)

Subscriptions cost £15.50 (except *Mettle*: £13.80) for one year for delivery within the UK. Please tick relevant boxes and fill in the form bel[ow]

☐ *Every Day with Jesus* (1yr, 6 issues)
☐ Large Print *Every Day with Jesus* (1yr, 6 issues)
☐ *Inspiring Women Every Day* (1yr, 6 issues)
☐ *Life Every Day* (Jeff Lucas) (1yr, 6 issues)

☐ *Cover to Cover Every Day* (1yr, 6 issues)
☐ *Mettle*: 14-18s (1yr, 3 issues)
☐ *YP's*: 11-15s (1yr, 6 issues)
☐ *Topz*: 7-11s (1yr, 6 issues)

Issue to commence fro[m]
☐ Jan/Feb ☐ Jul/Aug
☐ Mar/Apr ☐ Sep/Oct
☐ May/Jun ☐ Nov/Dec

CWR

Instruction to your Bank or Building Society to pay by Direct Debit

DIRECT Debit

Please fill in the form and send to: CWR, Waverley Abbey House, Waverley Lane, Farnham, Surrey GU9 8EP

Name and full postal address of your Bank or Building Society

To: The Manager _____ Bank/Building Society

Address _____
_____
_____ Postcode _____

Name(s) of Account Holder(s)
_____

Branch Sort Code
☐☐ ☐☐ ☐☐

Bank/Building Society account number
☐☐☐☐☐☐☐☐

Originator's Identification Number

4	2	0	4	8	7

Reference
☐☐☐☐☐☐☐☐☐☐☐☐☐☐

Instruction to your Bank or Building Society

Please pay CWR Direct Debits from the account detailed in this Instruction subje[ct] to the safeguards assured by the Direct Debit Guarantee.
I understand that this Instruction may remain with CWR and, if so, details will be passed electronically to my Bank/Building Society.

Signature(s)
_____

Date _____

Banks and Building Societies may not accept Direct Debit Instructions for some types of account